Individual Studies for Grade 6

*A Year of Lesson Plans
for Language Arts, Math, and Science*

by
Sonya Shafer

Individual Studies for Grade 6: A Year of Lesson Plans for Language Arts, Math, and Science
© 2016, Sonya Shafer

Cover Design: John Shafer and Sarah Shafer

ISBN 978-1-61634-347-7 printed
ISBN 978-1-61634-348-4 electronic download

Published by
Simply Charlotte Mason, LLC
930 New Hope Road #11-892
Lawrenceville, Georgia 30045
simplycharlottemason.com

Printed by PrintLogic, Inc.
Monroe, Georgia, USA

Contents

How to Use 7
Complete Year's Resources List 8

Term 1 9

    Lesson 1 11
    Lesson 2 11
    Lesson 3 11
    Lesson 4 11
    Lesson 5 12
    Lesson 6 12
    Lesson 7 12
    Lesson 8 13
    Lesson 9 13
    Lesson 10 13
    Lesson 11 13
    Lesson 12 14
    Lesson 13 14
    Lesson 14 14
    Lesson 15 15
    Lesson 16 15
    Lesson 17 16
    Lesson 18 16
    Lesson 19 16
    Lesson 20 16
    Lesson 21 17
    Lesson 22 17
    Lesson 23 17
    Lesson 24 17
    Lesson 25 18
    Lesson 26 18
    Lesson 27 18
    Lesson 28 19
    Lesson 29 19
    Lesson 30 19
    Lesson 31 19
    Lesson 32 20
    Lesson 33 20
    Lesson 34 20
    Lesson 35 21
    Lesson 36 21
    Lesson 37 21
    Lesson 38 21
    Lesson 39 22
    Lesson 40 22
    Lesson 41 22
    Lesson 42 22

Lesson 43 23
Lesson 44 23
Lesson 45 23
Lesson 46 24
Lesson 47 24
Lesson 48 24
Lesson 49 24
Lesson 50 25
Lesson 51 25
Lesson 52 25
Lesson 53 26
Lesson 54 26
Lesson 55 26
Lesson 56 26
Lesson 57 27
Lesson 58 27
Lesson 59 27
Lesson 60 28

Term 2 .... *29*
Lesson 61 31
Lesson 62 31
Lesson 63 32
Lesson 64 32
Lesson 65 32
Lesson 66 33
Lesson 67 34
Lesson 68 34
Lesson 69 34
Lesson 70 35
Lesson 71 35
Lesson 72 36
Lesson 73 36
Lesson 74 36
Lesson 75 37
Lesson 76 37
Lesson 77 38
Lesson 78 38
Lesson 79 39
Lesson 80 39
Lesson 81 39
Lesson 82 40
Lesson 83 40
Lesson 84 41
Lesson 85 41
Lesson 86 41
Lesson 87 42
Lesson 88 42
Lesson 89 43

Lesson 90 43
Lesson 91 44
Lesson 92 44
Lesson 93 45
Lesson 94 45
Lesson 95 45
Lesson 96 46
Lesson 97 46
Lesson 98 47
Lesson 99 47
Lesson 100 47
Lesson 101 48
Lesson 102 48
Lesson 103 49
Lesson 104 49
Lesson 105 50
Lesson 106 50
Lesson 107 51
Lesson 108 51
Lesson 109 51
Lesson 110 52
Lesson 111 52
Lesson 112 53
Lesson 113 53
Lesson 114 53
Lesson 115 53
Lesson 116 54
Lesson 117 54
Lesson 118 54
Lesson 119 55
Lesson 120 55

Term 3 .... *57*
Lesson 121 59
Lesson 122 59
Lesson 123 59
Lesson 124 60
Lesson 125 60
Lesson 126 60
Lesson 127 61
Lesson 128 61
Lesson 129 61
Lesson 130 62
Lesson 131 62
Lesson 132 62
Lesson 133 63
Lesson 134 63
Lesson 135 63
Lesson 136 64

Lesson 137 64
Lesson 138 64
Lesson 139 65
Lesson 140 65
Lesson 141 65
Lesson 142 66
Lesson 143 66
Lesson 144 66
Lesson 145 67
Lesson 146 67
Lesson 147 67
Lesson 148 68
Lesson 149 68
Lesson 150 68
Lesson 151 68
Lesson 152 69
Lesson 153 69
Lesson 154 69
Lesson 155 70
Lesson 156 70
Lesson 157 70
Lesson 158 70
Lesson 159 71
Lesson 160 71
Lesson 161 71
Lesson 162 71
Lesson 163 72
Lesson 164 72
Lesson 165 72
Lesson 166 73
Lesson 167 73
Lesson 168 73
Lesson 169 73
Lesson 170 74
Lesson 171 74
Lesson 172 74
Lesson 173 75
Lesson 174 75
Lesson 175 75
Lesson 176 75
Lesson 177 76
Lesson 178 76
Lesson 179 76
Lesson 180 77

How to Use

Most school subjects can be taught to your whole family together, but some subjects are best taught individually so you can progress at the student's pace. This book of lesson plans contains suggestions and assignments for individual work for students in grade 6. Complete one lesson plan per day to finish these studies in a school year.

The lesson plans in this book cover language arts, science, and math.

Language Arts

Students will continue a study of the parts of speech and progress in spelling, capitalization, punctuation, and English usage guidelines using the literary passages presented in *Spelling Wisdom, Book 2,* and the guided discovery lessons in *Using Language Well, Book 2*. The first half of these books was completed in grade 5; the rest will be covered this year.

Written narration will be assigned to encourage your student to continue to progress in capturing his thoughts on paper and applying guidelines he has learned about English grammar, usage, and mechanics. Rubrics and further instructions are provided in the *Using Language Well, Book 2, Teacher Guide and Answer Key*.

Science

Science can be done individually, or if you have more than one student in grades 1–6, they may all do one science course together. Simply Charlotte Mason has several to choose from.

Nature Study is an important part of science studies; be sure to include it. Follow the Nature Study suggestions in your selected science course or use the nature notebook, *Journaling a Year in Nature,* to guide your weekly study. Nature Study can be done all together as a family, but we have included reminders in these individual plans too.

Math

Use the math curriculum of your choice. These lesson plans will include reminders to work on it. As with other individual work, be sure to go at your student's pace.

Complete Year's Resources List

- *Spelling Wisdom, Book 2*
  Students will complete the last half of this book this year; the first half was covered in grade 5.
- *Using Language Well, Book 2, Student Book*
  Students will complete the last half of this book this year; the first half was covered in grade 5.
- *Using Language Well, Book 2, Teacher Guide and Answer Key*
- (optional) *Analytical Grammar,* Student Book and Teacher Book
- Simply Charlotte Mason (SCM) science course of choice
- *Journaling a Year in Nature* notebooks, one per person (optional)
- Math course of choice
- Typing course of choice

Note: All resources except math, typing, and Analytical Grammar *are available from Simply Charlotte Mason.* Analytical Grammar *can be found at http://analyticalgrammar.com.*

Term 1
(12 weeks; 5 lessons/week)

Term 1 Resources List

- *Spelling Wisdom, Book 2*
- *Using Language Well, Book 2, Student Book*
- *Using Language Well, Book 2, Teacher Guide and Answer Key*
- Simply Charlotte Mason (SCM) science course of choice
- *Journaling a Year in Nature* notebooks (optional)
- Typing course of choice
- Math course of choice

Weekly Schedule

Day One	Day Two	Day Three	Day Four	Day Five
Math (20–30 min.)	Math (20–30 min.)	Math (20–30 min.)	Math (20–30 min.)	Math (20–30 min.)
	Science (20–30 min.)		Science (20–30 min.)	(Nature Study)
Spelling Wisdom & Using Language Well (20–30 min.)		Typing (15–20 min.)	Spelling Wisdom & Using Language Well (20–30 min.)	

Lesson 1

Materials Needed
- Math course of choice *Delayed*
- *Spelling Wisdom, Book 2*
- *Using Language Well, Book 2, Student Book*
- *Using Language Well, Book 2, Teacher Guide and Answer Key*

Math: Work on your selected math curriculum for about 30 minutes.

Spelling and Grammar: Complete *Using Language Well, Book 2,* lesson 71.

Tip: The lessons assigned in Using Language Well, Book 2, *are designed to be completed independently. Check your student's work and oversee the dictation portion when he is ready. See the* Using Language Well, Book 2, Teacher Guide and Answer Key *for details.*

Lesson 2

Materials Needed
- SCM science course of choice
- Math course of choice

Science: In your SCM science course, complete the first assignment for Week 1.

Math: Work on your selected math curriculum for about 30 minutes.

Lesson 3

Materials Needed
- Math course of choice
- Typing course of choice

Math: Work on your selected math curriculum for about 30 minutes.

Typing: Work on your selected typing course for about 20 minutes.

Lesson 4

Materials Needed
- *Spelling Wisdom, Book 2*
- *Using Language Well, Book 2, Student Book*
- *Using Language Well, Book 2, Teacher Guide and Answer Key*
- SCM science course of choice
- Math course of choice

Notes

Violet

8/22/19

8/23/

VIOLET

8/28/19

8/29

Spelling and Grammar: Complete *Using Language Well, Book 2,* lesson 72.

Science: In your SCM science course, complete the second assignment for Week 1.

Math: Work on your selected math curriculum for about 30 minutes.

Lesson 5

Materials Needed
- Math course of choice
- *Journaling a Year in Nature* notebooks (optional)

Math: Work on your selected math curriculum for about 30 minutes.

Nature Study: Take the whole family outside for nature study.

Tip: Follow the Nature Study suggestions in your SCM science course or use the nature notebook, Journaling a Year in Nature, *to guide your weekly study.*

Lesson 6

Materials Needed
- Math course of choice
- *Spelling Wisdom, Book 2*
- *Using Language Well, Book 2, Student Book*
- *Using Language Well, Book 2, Teacher Guide and Answer Key*

Math: Work on your selected math curriculum for about 30 minutes.

Spelling and Grammar: Complete *Using Language Well, Book 2,* lesson 73.

Reminder: Assign your student to write one narration from his history, geography, Bible, or science readings this week. Use Rubric 2.3 from Using Language Well, Book 2, Teacher Guide and Answer Key *to help you evaluate his writing. Continue oral narrations daily.*

Lesson 7

Materials Needed
- SCM science course of choice
- Math course of choice

Science: In your SCM science course, complete the first assignment for Week 2.

Math: Work on your selected math curriculum for about 30 minutes.

Lesson 8

Materials Needed
- Math course of choice
- Typing course of choice

Math: Work on your selected math curriculum for about 30 minutes.

Typing: Work on your selected typing course for about 20 minutes.

Lesson 9

Materials Needed
- *Spelling Wisdom, Book 2*
- *Using Language Well, Book 2, Student Book*
- *Using Language Well, Book 2, Teacher Guide and Answer Key* — *Birds Together #3*
- SCM science course of choice
- Math course of choice *Review Lesson 6*

Spelling and Grammar: Complete *Using Language Well, Book 2,* lesson 74 ~~74~~ 75

Science: In your SCM science course, complete the second assignment for Week 2.

Math: Work on your selected math curriculum for about 30 minutes.

Lesson 10

Materials Needed
- Math course of choice
- *Journaling a Year in Nature* notebooks (optional)

Math: Work on your selected math curriculum for about 30 minutes.

Nature Study: Take the whole family outside for nature study.

Tip: Follow the Nature Study suggestions in your SCM science course or use the nature notebook, Journaling a Year in Nature, *to guide your weekly study.*

Lesson 11

Materials Needed
- Math course of choice

Notes

Violet
9/5

9/6

9/11

Notes

- *Spelling Wisdom, Book 2*
- *Using Language Well, Book 2, Student Book*
- *Using Language Well, Book 2, Teacher Guide and Answer Key*

Math: Work on your selected math curriculum for about 30 minutes.

Spelling and Grammar: Complete *Using Language Well, Book 2,* lesson 75.

Reminder: Assign your student to write one narration from his history, geography, Bible, or science readings this week. Use Rubric 2.3 from Using Language Well, Book 2, Teacher Guide and Answer Key *to help you evaluate his writing. Continue oral narrations daily.*

Lesson 12

Materials Needed
- SCM science course of choice
- Math course of choice

Science: In your SCM science course, complete the first assignment for Week 3.

Math: Work on your selected math curriculum for about 30 minutes.

Lesson 13

Materials Needed
- Math course of choice
- Typing course of choice

Math: Work on your selected math curriculum for about 30 minutes.

Typing: Work on your selected typing course for about 20 minutes.

Tip: If your student would like to, encourage him to keep a Book of Mottoes, or a commonplace book,—a journal in which he records personally selected quotations, poetry, excerpts, or Scripture passages that are meaningful to him. You might allow him to purchase a special journal for this ongoing project. You will see periodic reminders in these lesson plans; mention them only if your student is interested.

Lesson 14

Materials Needed
- *Spelling Wisdom, Book 2*

- *Using Language Well, Book 2, Student Book*
- *Using Language Well, Book 2, Teacher Guide and Answer Key*
- SCM science course of choice
- Math course of choice

Spelling and Grammar: Complete *Using Language Well, Book 2*, lesson 76.

Science: In your SCM science course, complete the second assignment for Week 3.

Math: Work on your selected math curriculum for about 30 minutes.

Lesson 15

Materials Needed
- Math course of choice
- *Journaling a Year in Nature* notebooks (optional)

Math: Work on your selected math curriculum for about 30 minutes.

Nature Study: Take the whole family outside for nature study.

Tip: Follow the Nature Study suggestions in your SCM science course or use the nature notebook, Journaling a Year in Nature, *to guide your weekly study.*

Lesson 16

Materials Needed
- Math course of choice
- *Spelling Wisdom, Book 2*
- *Using Language Well, Book 2, Student Book*
- *Using Language Well, Book 2, Teacher Guide and Answer Key*

Math: Work on your selected math curriculum for about 30 minutes.

Spelling and Grammar: Complete *Using Language Well, Book 2*, lesson 77.

Reminder: Assign your student to write one narration from his history, geography, Bible, or science readings this week. Use Rubric 2.4 from Using Language Well, Book 2, Teacher Guide and Answer Key *to help you evaluate his writing. Continue oral narrations daily.*

9/17/19

9/18

9/18

Lesson 17

Materials Needed
- SCM science course of choice
- Math course of choice

Science: In your SCM science course, complete the first assignment for Week 4.

Math: Work on your selected math curriculum for about 30 minutes.

Lesson 18

Materials Needed
- Math course of choice
- Typing course of choice

Math: Work on your selected math curriculum for about 30 minutes.

Typing: Work on your selected typing course for about 20 minutes.

Lesson 19

Materials Needed
- *Spelling Wisdom, Book 2*
- *Using Language Well, Book 2, Student Book*
- *Using Language Well, Book 2, Teacher Guide and Answer Key*
- SCM science course of choice
- Math course of choice

Spelling and Grammar: Complete *Using Language Well, Book 2,* lesson 78.

Science: In your SCM science course, complete the second assignment for Week 4.

Math: Work on your selected math curriculum for about 30 minutes.

Lesson 20

Materials Needed
- Math course of choice
- *Journaling a Year in Nature* notebooks (optional)

Math: Work on your selected math curriculum for about 30 minutes.

Nature Study: Take the whole family outside for nature study.

9/23

Lesson 21

Materials Needed
- Math course of choice
- *Spelling Wisdom, Book 2*
- *Using Language Well, Book 2, Student Book*
- *Using Language Well, Book 2, Teacher Guide and Answer Key*

Math: Work on your selected math curriculum for about 30 minutes.

Spelling and Grammar: Complete *Using Language Well, Book 2,* lesson 79.

9/24/19

Reminder: Assign your student to write one narration from his history, geography, Bible, or science readings this week. Use Rubric 2.4 from Using Language Well, Book 2, Teacher Guide and Answer Key *to help you evaluate his writing. Continue oral narrations daily.*

Lesson 22

Materials Needed
- SCM science course of choice
- Math course of choice

Science: In your SCM science course, complete the first assignment for Week 5.

Math: Work on your selected math curriculum for about 30 minutes.

Lesson 23

Materials Needed
- Math course of choice
- Typing course of choice

Math: Work on your selected math curriculum for about 30 minutes.

Typing: Work on your selected typing course for about 20 minutes.

Lesson 24

Materials Needed
- *Spelling Wisdom, Book 2*
- *Using Language Well, Book 2, Student Book*
- *Using Language Well, Book 2, Teacher Guide and Answer Key*
- SCM science course of choice
- Math course of choice

VIOLET

Notes 9/25/19

Spelling and Grammar: Complete *Using Language Well, Book 2,* lesson 80.

Science: In your SCM science course, complete the second assignment for Week 5.

Math: Work on your selected math curriculum for about 30 minutes.

Lesson 25

9/27

Materials Needed
- Math course of choice
- *Journaling a Year in Nature* notebooks (optional)

Math: Work on your selected math curriculum for about 30 minutes.

Nature Study: Take the whole family outside for nature study.

Lesson 26

9/27

Materials Needed
- Math course of choice
- *Spelling Wisdom, Book 2*
- *Using Language Well, Book 2, Student Book*
- *Using Language Well, Book 2, Teacher Guide and Answer Key*

Math: Work on your selected math curriculum for about 30 minutes.

Spelling and Grammar: Complete *Using Language Well, Book 2,* lesson 81.

Reminder: Assign your student to write one narration from his history, geography, Bible, or science readings this week. Use Rubric 2.4 from Using Language Well, Book 2, Teacher Guide and Answer Key *to help you evaluate his writing. Continue oral narrations daily.*

Lesson 27

Materials Needed
- SCM science course of choice
- Math course of choice

Science: In your SCM science course, complete the first assignment for Week 6.

Math: Work on your selected math curriculum for about 30 minutes.

Lesson 28

Materials Needed
- Math course of choice
- Typing course of choice

Math: Work on your selected math curriculum for about 30 minutes.

Typing: Work on your selected typing course for about 20 minutes.

Tip: Remind your student to record in his Book of Mottoes any meaningful quotations, poetry, excerpts, or Scripture passages from recent readings (if he is interested in that ongoing project).

Lesson 29

Materials Needed
- *Spelling Wisdom, Book 2*
- *Using Language Well, Book 2, Student Book*
- *Using Language Well, Book 2, Teacher Guide and Answer Key*
- SCM science course of choice
- Math course of choice

Spelling and Grammar: Complete *Using Language Well, Book 2,* lesson 82.

Science: In your SCM science course, complete the second assignment for Week 6.

Math: Work on your selected math curriculum for about 30 minutes.

Lesson 30

Materials Needed
- Math course of choice
- *Journaling a Year in Nature* notebooks (optional)

Math: Work on your selected math curriculum for about 30 minutes.

Nature Study: Take the whole family outside for nature study.

Lesson 31

Materials Needed
- Math course of choice
- *Spelling Wisdom, Book 2*
- *Using Language Well, Book 2, Student Book*

Notes

10/3

10/3

10/9

Violet

Notes

    • *Using Language Well, Book 2, Teacher Guide and Answer Key*

Math: Work on your selected math curriculum for about 30 minutes.

Spelling and Grammar: Complete *Using Language Well, Book 2,* lesson 83.

Reminder: Assign your student to write one narration from his history, geography, Bible, or science readings this week. Use Rubric 2.4 from Using Language Well, Book 2, Teacher Guide and Answer Key *to help you evaluate his writing. Continue oral narrations daily.*

Lesson 32

Materials Needed
- SCM science course of choice
- Math course of choice

Science: In your SCM science course, complete the first assignment for Week 7.

Math: Work on your selected math curriculum for about 30 minutes.

Lesson 33

Materials Needed
- Math course of choice
- Typing course of choice

11|9

Math: Work on your selected math curriculum for about 30 minutes.

Typing: Work on your selected typing course for about 20 minutes.

Lesson 34

Materials Needed
- *Spelling Wisdom, Book 2*
- *Using Language Well, Book 2, Student Book*
- *Using Language Well, Book 2, Teacher Guide and Answer Key*
- SCM science course of choice
- Math course of choice

11|11

Spelling and Grammar: Complete *Using Language Well, Book 2,* lesson 84.

Science: In your SCM science course, complete the second assignment for Week 7.

Math: Work on your selected math curriculum for about 30 minutes.

Lesson 35

Materials Needed
- Math course of choice
- *Journaling a Year in Nature* notebooks (optional)

Math: Work on your selected math curriculum for about 30 minutes.

Nature Study: Take the whole family outside for nature study.

Lesson 36

Materials Needed
- Math course of choice
- *Spelling Wisdom, Book 2*
- *Using Language Well, Book 2, Student Book*
- *Using Language Well, Book 2, Teacher Guide and Answer Key*

Math: Work on your selected math curriculum for about 30 minutes.

Spelling and Grammar: Complete *Using Language Well, Book 2,* lesson 85.

Reminder: Assign your student to write one narration from his history, geography, Bible, or science readings this week. Use Rubric 2.4 from Using Language Well, Book 2, Teacher Guide and Answer Key *to help you evaluate his writing. Continue oral narrations daily.*

Lesson 37

Materials Needed
- SCM science course of choice
- Math course of choice

Science: In your SCM science course, complete the first assignment for Week 8.

Math: Work on your selected math curriculum for about 30 minutes.

Lesson 38

Materials Needed
- Math course of choice
- Typing course of choice

Math: Work on your selected math curriculum for about 30 minutes.

Typing: Work on your selected typing course for about 20 minutes.

11/13

Notes

Lesson 39

Materials Needed
- *Spelling Wisdom, Book 2*
- *Using Language Well, Book 2, Student Book*
- *Using Language Well, Book 2, Teacher Guide and Answer Key*
- SCM science course of choice
- Math course of choice

Spelling and Grammar: Complete *Using Language Well, Book 2,* lesson 86.

Science: In your SCM science course, complete the second assignment for Week 8.

Math: Work on your selected math curriculum for about 30 minutes.

Lesson 40

Materials Needed
- Math course of choice
- *Journaling a Year in Nature* notebooks (optional)

Math: Work on your selected math curriculum for about 30 minutes.

Nature Study: Take the whole family outside for nature study.

Lesson 41

Materials Needed
- Math course of choice
- *Spelling Wisdom, Book 2*
- *Using Language Well, Book 2, Student Book*
- *Using Language Well, Book 2, Teacher Guide and Answer Key*

Math: Work on your selected math curriculum for about 30 minutes.

Spelling and Grammar: Complete *Using Language Well, Book 2,* lesson 87.

Reminder: Assign your student to write one narration from his history, geography, Bible, or science readings this week. Use Rubric 2.4 from Using Language Well, Book 2, Teacher Guide and Answer Key *to help you evaluate his writing. Continue oral narrations daily.*

Lesson 42

Materials Needed
- SCM science course of choice

- Math course of choice

Science: In your SCM science course, complete the first assignment for Week 9.

Math: Work on your selected math curriculum for about 30 minutes.

Lesson 43

Materials Needed
- Math course of choice
- Typing course of choice

Math: Work on your selected math curriculum for about 30 minutes.

Typing: Work on your selected typing course for about 20 minutes.

Tip: Remind your student to record in his Book of Mottoes any meaningful quotations, poetry, excerpts, or Scripture passages from recent readings (if he is interested in that ongoing project).

Lesson 44

Materials Needed
- *Spelling Wisdom, Book 2*
- *Using Language Well, Book 2, Student Book*
- *Using Language Well, Book 2, Teacher Guide and Answer Key*
- SCM science course of choice
- Math course of choice

Spelling and Grammar: Complete *Using Language Well, Book 2,* lesson 88.

Science: In your SCM science course, complete the second assignment for Week 9.

Math: Work on your selected math curriculum for about 30 minutes.

Lesson 45

Materials Needed
- Math course of choice
- *Journaling a Year in Nature* notebooks (optional)

Math: Work on your selected math curriculum for about 30 minutes.

Nature Study: Take the whole family outside for nature study.

Lesson 46

Materials Needed
- Math course of choice
- *Spelling Wisdom, Book 2*
- *Using Language Well, Book 2, Student Book*
- *Using Language Well, Book 2, Teacher Guide and Answer Key*

Math: Work on your selected math curriculum for about 30 minutes.

Spelling and Grammar: Complete *Using Language Well, Book 2,* lesson 89.

Reminder: Assign your student to write one narration from his history, geography, Bible, or science readings this week. Use Rubric 2.4 from Using Language Well, Book 2, Teacher Guide and Answer Key *to help you evaluate his writing. Continue oral narrations daily.*

Lesson 47

Materials Needed
- SCM science course of choice
- Math course of choice

Science: In your SCM science course, complete the first assignment for Week 10.

Math: Work on your selected math curriculum for about 30 minutes.

Lesson 48

Materials Needed
- Math course of choice
- Typing course of choice

Math: Work on your selected math curriculum for about 30 minutes.

Typing: Work on your selected typing course for about 20 minutes.

Reminder: Get Analytical Grammar *for Term 2 if you want to add more in-depth grammar study.*

Lesson 49

Materials Needed
- *Spelling Wisdom, Book 2*

- *Using Language Well, Book 2, Student Book*
- *Using Language Well, Book 2, Teacher Guide and Answer Key*
- SCM science course of choice
- Math course of choice

Spelling and Grammar: Complete *Using Language Well, Book 2,* lesson 90.

Science: In your SCM science course, complete the second assignment for Week 10.

Math: Work on your selected math curriculum for about 30 minutes.

Lesson 50

Materials Needed
- Math course of choice
- *Journaling a Year in Nature* notebooks (optional)

Math: Work on your selected math curriculum for about 30 minutes.

Nature Study: Take the whole family outside for nature study.

Lesson 51

Materials Needed
- Math course of choice
- *Spelling Wisdom, Book 2*
- *Using Language Well, Book 2, Student Book*
- *Using Language Well, Book 2, Teacher Guide and Answer Key*

Math: Work on your selected math curriculum for about 30 minutes.

Spelling and Grammar: Complete *Using Language Well, Book 2,* lesson 91.

Reminder: Assign your student to write one narration from his history, geography, Bible, or science readings this week. Use Rubric 2.4 from Using Language Well, Book 2, Teacher Guide and Answer Key *to help you evaluate his writing. Continue oral narrations daily.*

Lesson 52

Materials Needed
- SCM science course of choice
- Math course of choice

Science: In your SCM science course, complete the first assignment for Week 11.

Math: Work on your selected math curriculum for about 30 minutes.

Lesson 53

Materials Needed
- Math course of choice
- Typing course of choice

Math: Work on your selected math curriculum for about 30 minutes.

Typing: Work on your selected typing course for about 20 minutes.

Lesson 54

Materials Needed
- *Spelling Wisdom, Book 2*
- *Using Language Well, Book 2, Student Book*
- *Using Language Well, Book 2, Teacher Guide and Answer Key*
- SCM science course of choice
- Math course of choice

Spelling and Grammar: Complete *Using Language Well, Book 2,* lesson 92.

Science: In your SCM science course, complete the second assignment for Week 11.

Math: Work on your selected math curriculum for about 30 minutes.

Lesson 55

Materials Needed
- Math course of choice
- *Journaling a Year in Nature* notebooks (optional)

Math: Work on your selected math curriculum for about 30 minutes.

Nature Study: Take the whole family outside for nature study.

Lesson 56

Materials Needed
- Math course of choice
- *Spelling Wisdom, Book 2*
- *Using Language Well, Book 2, Student Book*
- *Using Language Well, Book 2, Teacher Guide and Answer Key*

Math: Work on your selected math curriculum for about 30 minutes.

Spelling and Grammar: Complete *Using Language Well, Book 2,* lesson 93.

Reminder: Assign your student to write one narration from his history, geography, Bible, or science readings this week. Use Rubric 2.4 from Using Language Well, Book 2, Teacher Guide and Answer Key *to help you evaluate his writing. Continue oral narrations daily.*

Lesson 57

Materials Needed
- SCM science course of choice
- Math course of choice

Science: In your SCM science course, complete the first assignment for Week 12.

Math: Work on your selected math curriculum for about 30 minutes.

Lesson 58

Materials Needed
- Math course of choice
- Typing course of choice

Math: Work on your selected math curriculum for about 30 minutes.

Typing: Work on your selected typing course for about 20 minutes.

Tip: Remind your student to record in his Book of Mottoes any meaningful quotations, poetry, excerpts, or Scripture passages from recent readings (if he is interested in that ongoing project).

Lesson 59

Materials Needed
- *Spelling Wisdom, Book 2*
- *Using Language Well, Book 2, Student Book*
- *Using Language Well, Book 2, Teacher Guide and Answer Key*
- SCM science course of choice
- Math course of choice

Spelling and Grammar: Complete *Using Language Well, Book 2,* lesson 94.

Science: In your SCM science course, complete the second assignment for Week 12.

Math: Work on your selected math curriculum for about 30 minutes.

Lesson 60

Materials Needed
- Math course of choice
- *Journaling a Year in Nature* notebooks (optional)

Math: Work on your selected math curriculum for about 30 minutes.

Nature Study: Take the whole family outside for nature study.

Term 2

(12 weeks; 5 lessons/week)

Term 2 Resources List

- *Spelling Wisdom, Book 2*
- *Using Language Well, Book 2, Student Book*
- *Using Language Well, Book 2, Teacher Guide and Answer Key*
- (optional) *Analytical Grammar*, Student Book and Teacher Book
- Simply Charlotte Mason (SCM) science course of choice
- *Journaling a Year in Nature* notebooks (optional)
- Typing course of choice
- Math course of choice

Weekly Schedule

	Day One	Day Two	Day Three	Day Four	Day Five
	Math (20–30 min.)	Math (20–30 min.)	Math (20–30 min.)	Math (20–30 min.)	Math (20–30 min.)
	(Nature Study)		Science (20–30 min.)		Science (20–30 min.)
		Spelling Wisdom & Using Language Well (20–30 min.)		Typing (15–20 min.)	Spelling Wisdom & Using Language Well (20–30 min.)
Schedule A	(opt.) Analytical Grammar	(opt.) Analytical Grammar	(opt.) Analytical Grammar	(opt.) Analytical Grammar	(opt.) Analytical Grammar
Schedule B	(opt.) Analytical Grammar		(opt.) Analytical Grammar	(opt.) Analytical Grammar	

Note: For those who would like more in-depth grammar study, including diagramming sentences, optional plans are given for adding the first portion of *Analytical Grammar,* a three-year course. Select whether you want to follow Schedule A or Schedule B to work through the units for this year. Follow the Schedule A plan to complete the assigned units in ten weeks. Students following Schedule A will be asked to complete assignments from both *Analytical Grammar* and *Using Language Well* on some days. Follow the Schedule B plan to spread out the lessons. Students following Schedule B will be asked to complete an assignment from either *Analytical Grammar* or *Using Language Well* on given days, but not both on the same day.

Lesson 61

Materials Needed
- Math course of choice
- (optional) *Analytical Grammar,* Student Book and Teacher Book (Schedules A and B)
- *Journaling a Year in Nature* notebooks (optional)

Math: Work on your selected math curriculum for about 30 minutes.

(optional) Analytical Grammar, Schedule A: Go over Unit 1, "Nouns, Articles, & Adjectives," notes with your student (or use the DVD companion). Do the first two sentences of Unit 1, Exercise 1, together, then assign the remainder to be done independently.

(optional) Analytical Grammar, Schedule B: Go over Unit 1, "Nouns, Articles, & Adjectives," notes with your student (or use the DVD companion). Do the first two sentences of Unit 1, Exercise 1, together, then assign the remainder to be done independently.

Nature Study: Take the whole family outside for nature study.

Reminder: Assign your student to write one narration from his history, geography, Bible, or science readings this week. Use Rubric 2.4 from Using Language Well, Book 2, Teacher Guide and Answer Key *to help you evaluate his writing. Continue oral narrations daily.*

Lesson 62

Materials Needed
- *Spelling Wisdom, Book 2*
- *Using Language Well, Book 2, Student Book*
- *Using Language Well, Book 2, Teacher Guide and Answer Key*
- Math course of choice
- (optional) *Analytical Grammar,* Student Book and Teacher Book (Schedule A)

Spelling and Grammar: Complete *Using Language Well, Book 2,* lesson 95.

Math: Work on your selected math curriculum for about 30 minutes.

(optional) Analytical Grammar, Schedule A: Go over the completed Unit 1, Exercise 1, together, then assign Exercise 2 to be done independently.

Lesson 63

Materials Needed
- (optional) *Analytical Grammar,* Student Book and Teacher Book (Schedules A and B)
- SCM science course of choice
- Math course of choice

(optional) Analytical Grammar, Schedule A: Go over the completed Unit 1, Exercise 2, together, then assign Exercise 3 to be done independently.

(optional) Analytical Grammar, Schedule B: Go over the completed Unit 1, Exercise 1, together, then assign Exercise 2 to be done independently.

Science: In your SCM science course, complete the first assignment for Week 13.

Math: Work on your selected math curriculum for about 30 minutes.

Lesson 64

Materials Needed
- Typing course of choice
- Math course of choice
- (optional) *Analytical Grammar,* Student Book and Teacher Book (Schedules A and B)

Typing: Work on your selected typing course for about 20 minutes.

Math: Work on your selected math curriculum for about 30 minutes.

(optional) Analytical Grammar, Schedule A: Go over the completed Unit 1, Exercise 3, together. Assign and go over the Skills Support exercise if desired.

Tip: Your student will be getting plenty of writing experience through the written narrations assigned in other subjects, as explained in the Using Language Well Teacher Guide. *The Skills Support exercises in* Analytical Grammar *are not necessary, but you may include them if desired.*

(optional) Analytical Grammar, Schedule B: Go over the completed Unit 1, Exercise 2, together, then assign Exercise 3 to be done independently.

Lesson 65

Materials Needed
- SCM science course of choice
- *Spelling Wisdom, Book 2*

- *Using Language Well, Book 2, Student Book*
- *Using Language Well, Book 2, Teacher Guide and Answer Key*
- Math course of choice
- (optional) *Analytical Grammar,* Student Book and Teacher Book (Schedule A)

Science: In your SCM science course, complete the second assignment for Week 13.

Spelling and Grammar: Complete *Using Language Well, Book 2,* lesson 96.

Math: Work on your selected math curriculum for about 30 minutes.

(optional) Analytical Grammar, Schedule A: Assign the Unit 1 test, allowing your student to use his notes as he works. Go over the test together.

Lesson 66

Materials Needed
- Math course of choice
- (optional) *Analytical Grammar,* Student Book and Teacher Book (Schedules A and B)
- *Journaling a Year in Nature* notebooks (optional)

Math: Work on your selected math curriculum for about 30 minutes.

(optional) Analytical Grammar, Schedule A: Go over Unit 2, "Pronouns," notes with your student (or use the DVD companion). Do the first two sentences of Unit 2, Exercise 1, together, then assign the remainder to be done independently.

(optional) Analytical Grammar, Schedule B: Go over the completed Unit 1, Exercise 3, together. Assign and go over the Skills Support exercise if desired.

Tip: Your student will be getting plenty of writing experience through the written narrations assigned in other subjects, as explained in the Using Language Well Teacher Guide. *The Skills Support exercises in* Analytical Grammar *are not necessary, but you may include them if desired.*

Nature Study: Take the whole family outside for nature study.

Reminder: Assign your student to write one narration from his history, geography, Bible, or science readings this week. Use Rubric 2.4 from Using Language Well, Book 2, Teacher Guide and Answer Key *to help you evaluate his writing. Continue oral narrations daily.*

Lesson 67

Materials Needed

- *Spelling Wisdom, Book 2*
- *Using Language Well, Book 2, Student Book*
- *Using Language Well, Book 2, Teacher Guide and Answer Key*
- Math course of choice
- (optional) *Analytical Grammar,* Student Book and Teacher Book (Schedule A)

Spelling and Grammar: Complete *Using Language Well, Book 2,* lesson 97.

Math: Work on your selected math curriculum for about 30 minutes.

(optional) Analytical Grammar, Schedule A: Go over the completed Unit 2, Exercise 1, together, then assign Exercise 2 to be done independently.

Lesson 68

Materials Needed

- (optional) *Analytical Grammar,* Student Book and Teacher Book (Schedules A and B)
- SCM science course of choice
- Math course of choice

(optional) Analytical Grammar, Schedule A: Go over the completed Unit 2, Exercise 2, together, then assign Exercise 3 to be done independently.

(optional) Analytical Grammar, Schedule B: Assign the Unit 1 test, allowing your student to use his notes as he works. Go over the test together.

Science: In your SCM science course, complete the first assignment for Week 14.

Math: Work on your selected math curriculum for about 30 minutes.

Lesson 69

Materials Needed

- Typing course of choice
- Math course of choice
- (optional) *Analytical Grammar,* Student Book and Teacher Book (Schedules A and B)

Typing: Work on your selected typing course for about 20 minutes.

Math: Work on your selected math curriculum for about 30 minutes.

(optional) Analytical Grammar, Schedule A: Go over the completed Unit 2,

Exercise 3, together. Assign and go over the Skills Support exercise if desired.

(optional) Analytical Grammar, Schedule B: Go over Unit 2, "Pronouns," notes with your student (or use the DVD companion). Do the first two sentences of Unit 2, Exercise 1, together, then assign the remainder to be done independently.

Lesson 70

Materials Needed
- SCM science course of choice
- *Spelling Wisdom, Book 2*
- *Using Language Well, Book 2, Student Book*
- *Using Language Well, Book 2, Teacher Guide and Answer Key*
- Math course of choice
- (optional) *Analytical Grammar,* Student Book and Teacher Book (Schedule A)

Science: In your SCM science course, complete the second assignment for Week 14.

Spelling and Grammar: Complete *Using Language Well, Book 2,* lesson 98.

Math: Work on your selected math curriculum for about 30 minutes.

(optional) Analytical Grammar, Schedule A: Assign the Unit 2 test, allowing your student to use his notes as he works. Go over the test together.

Lesson 71

Materials Needed
- Math course of choice
- (optional) *Analytical Grammar,* Student Book and Teacher Book (Schedules A and B)
- *Journaling a Year in Nature* notebooks (optional)

Math: Work on your selected math curriculum for about 30 minutes.

(optional) Analytical Grammar, Schedule A: Go over Unit 3, "Prepositional Phrases," notes with your student (or use the DVD companion). Do the first two sentences of Unit 3, Exercise 1, together, then assign the remainder to be done independently.

(optional) Analytical Grammar, Schedule B: Go over the completed Unit 2, Exercise 1, together, then assign Exercise 2 to be done independently.

Nature Study: Take the whole family outside for nature study.

_____

Reminder: Assign your student to write one narration from his history, geography, Bible, or science readings this week. Use Rubric 2.4 from Using Language Well, Book 2, Teacher Guide and Answer Key *to help you evaluate his writing. Continue oral narrations daily.*

Lesson 72

Materials Needed
- *Spelling Wisdom, Book 2*
- *Using Language Well, Book 2, Student Book*
- *Using Language Well, Book 2, Teacher Guide and Answer Key*
- Math course of choice
- (optional) *Analytical Grammar,* Student Book and Teacher Book (Schedule A)

Spelling and Grammar: Complete *Using Language Well, Book 2,* lesson 99.

Math: Work on your selected math curriculum for about 30 minutes.

(optional) Analytical Grammar, Schedule A: Go over the completed Unit 3, Exercise 1, together, then assign Exercise 2 to be done independently.

Lesson 73

Materials Needed
- (optional) *Analytical Grammar,* Student Book and Teacher Book (Schedules A and B)
- SCM science course of choice
- Math course of choice

(optional) Analytical Grammar, Schedule A: Go over the completed Unit 3, Exercise 2, together, then assign Exercise 3 to be done independently.

(optional) Analytical Grammar, Schedule B: Go over the completed Unit 2, Exercise 2, together, then assign Exercise 3 to be done independently.

Science: In your SCM science course, complete the first assignment for Week 15.

Math: Work on your selected math curriculum for about 30 minutes.

Lesson 74

Materials Needed
- Typing course of choice
- Math course of choice
- (optional) *Analytical Grammar,* Student Book and Teacher Book (Schedules A and B)

Typing: Work on your selected typing course for about 20 minutes.

Math: Work on your selected math curriculum for about 30 minutes.

(optional) Analytical Grammar, Schedule A: Go over the completed Unit 3, Exercise 3, together. Assign and go over the Skills Support exercise if desired.

(optional) Analytical Grammar, Schedule B: Go over the completed Unit 2, Exercise 3, together. Assign and go over the Skills Support exercise if desired.

Lesson 75

Materials Needed
- SCM science course of choice
- *Spelling Wisdom, Book 2*
- *Using Language Well, Book 2, Student Book*
- *Using Language Well, Book 2, Teacher Guide and Answer Key*
- Math course of choice
- (optional) *Analytical Grammar,* Student Book and Teacher Book (Schedule A)

Science: In your SCM science course, complete the second assignment for Week 15.

Spelling and Grammar: Complete *Using Language Well, Book 2,* lesson 100.

Math: Work on your selected math curriculum for about 30 minutes.

(optional) Analytical Grammar, Schedule A: Assign the Unit 3 test, allowing your student to use his notes as he works. Go over the test together.

Tip: Remind your student to record in his Book of Mottoes any meaningful quotations, poetry, excerpts, or Scripture passages from recent readings (if he is interested in that ongoing project).

Lesson 76

Materials Needed
- Math course of choice
- (optional) *Analytical Grammar,* Student Book and Teacher Book (Schedules A and B)
- *Journaling a Year in Nature* notebooks (optional)

Math: Work on your selected math curriculum for about 30 minutes.

(optional) Analytical Grammar, Schedule A: Go over Unit 4, "Subject & Verb," notes with your student (or use the DVD companion). Do the first two

Notes

sentences of Unit 4, Exercise 1, together, then assign the remainder to be done independently.

(optional) Analytical Grammar, Schedule B: Assign the Unit 2 test, allowing your student to use his notes as he works. Go over the test together.

Nature Study: Take the whole family outside for nature study.

Reminder: Assign your student to write one narration from his history, geography, Bible, or science readings this week. Use Rubric 2.4 from Using Language Well, Book 2, Teacher Guide and Answer Key *to help you evaluate his writing. Continue oral narrations daily.*

Lesson 77

Materials Needed
- *Spelling Wisdom, Book 2*
- *Using Language Well, Book 2, Student Book*
- *Using Language Well, Book 2, Teacher Guide and Answer Key*
- Math course of choice
- (optional) *Analytical Grammar,* Student Book and Teacher Book (Schedule A)

Spelling and Grammar: Complete *Using Language Well, Book 2,* lesson 101.

Math: Work on your selected math curriculum for about 30 minutes.

(optional) Analytical Grammar, Schedule A: Go over the completed Unit 4, Exercise 1, together, then assign Exercise 2 to be done independently.

Lesson 78

Materials Needed
- (optional) *Analytical Grammar,* Student Book and Teacher Book (Schedules A and B)
- SCM science course of choice
- Math course of choice

(optional) Analytical Grammar, Schedule A: Go over the completed Unit 4, Exercise 2, together, then assign Exercise 3 to be done independently.

(optional) Analytical Grammar, Schedule B: Go over Unit 3, "Prepositional Phrases," notes with your student (or use the DVD companion). Do the first two sentences of Unit 3, Exercise 1, together, then assign the remainder to be done independently.

Science: In your SCM science course, complete the first assignment for Week 16.

Math: Work on your selected math curriculum for about 30 minutes.

Lesson 79

Materials Needed
- Typing course of choice
- Math course of choice
- (optional) *Analytical Grammar,* Student Book and Teacher Book (Schedules A and B)

Typing: Work on your selected typing course for about 20 minutes.

Math: Work on your selected math curriculum for about 30 minutes.

(optional) Analytical Grammar, Schedule A: Go over the completed Unit 4, Exercise 3, together. Assign and go over the Skills Support exercise if desired.

(optional) Analytical Grammar, Schedule B: Go over the completed Unit 3, Exercise 1, together, then assign Exercise 2 to be done independently.

Lesson 80

Materials Needed
- SCM science course of choice
- *Spelling Wisdom, Book 2*
- *Using Language Well, Book 2, Student Book*
- *Using Language Well, Book 2, Teacher Guide and Answer Key*
- Math course of choice
- (optional) *Analytical Grammar,* Student Book and Teacher Book (Schedule A)

Science: In your SCM science course, complete the second assignment for Week 16.

Spelling and Grammar: Complete *Using Language Well, Book 2,* lesson 102.

Math: Work on your selected math curriculum for about 30 minutes.

(optional) Analytical Grammar, Schedule A: Assign the Unit 4 test, allowing your student to use his notes as he works. Go over the test together.

Lesson 81

Materials Needed
- Math course of choice
- (optional) *Analytical Grammar,* Student Book and Teacher Book (Schedules A and B)
- *Journaling a Year in Nature* notebooks (optional)

Notes

Math: Work on your selected math curriculum for about 30 minutes.

(optional) Analytical Grammar, Schedule A: Go over Unit 5, "Adverbs," notes with your student (or use the DVD companion). Do the first two sentences of Unit 5, Exercise 1, together, then assign the remainder to be done independently.

(optional) Analytical Grammar, Schedule B: Go over the completed Unit 3, Exercise 2, together, then assign Exercise 3 to be done independently.

Nature Study: Take the whole family outside for nature study.

Reminder: Assign your student to write one narration from his history, geography, Bible, or science readings this week. Use Rubric 2.4 from Using Language Well, Book 2, Teacher Guide and Answer Key *to help you evaluate his writing. Continue oral narrations daily.*

Lesson 82

Materials Needed
- *Spelling Wisdom, Book 2*
- *Using Language Well, Book 2, Student Book*
- *Using Language Well, Book 2, Teacher Guide and Answer Key*
- Math course of choice
- (optional) *Analytical Grammar,* Student Book and Teacher Book (Schedule A)

Spelling and Grammar: Complete *Using Language Well, Book 2,* lesson 103.

Math: Work on your selected math curriculum for about 30 minutes.

(optional) Analytical Grammar, Schedule A: Go over the completed Unit 5, Exercise 1, together, then assign Exercise 2 to be done independently.

Lesson 83

Materials Needed
- (optional) *Analytical Grammar,* Student Book and Teacher Book (Schedules A and B)
- SCM science course of choice
- Math course of choice

(optional) Analytical Grammar, Schedule A: Go over the completed Unit 5, Exercise 2, together, then assign Exercise 3 to be done independently.

(optional) Analytical Grammar, Schedule B: Go over the completed Unit 3, Exercise 3, together. Assign and go over the Skills Support exercise if desired.

Science: In your SCM science course, complete the first assignment for Week 17.

Math: Work on your selected math curriculum for about 30 minutes.

Lesson 84

Materials Needed
- Typing course of choice
- Math course of choice
- (optional) *Analytical Grammar,* Student Book and Teacher Book (Schedules A and B)

Typing: Work on your selected typing course for about 20 minutes.

Math: Work on your selected math curriculum for about 30 minutes.

(optional) Analytical Grammar, Schedule A: Go over the completed Unit 5, Exercise 3, together. Assign and go over the Skills Support exercise if desired.

(optional) Analytical Grammar, Schedule B: Assign the Unit 3 test, allowing your student to use his notes as he works. Go over the test together.

Lesson 85

Materials Needed
- SCM science course of choice
- *Spelling Wisdom, Book 2*
- *Using Language Well, Book 2, Student Book*
- *Using Language Well, Book 2, Teacher Guide and Answer Key*
- Math course of choice
- (optional) *Analytical Grammar,* Student Book and Teacher Book (Schedule A)

Science: In your SCM science course, complete the second assignment for Week 17.

Spelling and Grammar: Complete *Using Language Well, Book 2,* lesson 104.

Math: Work on your selected math curriculum for about 30 minutes.

(optional) Analytical Grammar, Schedule A: Assign the Unit 5 test, allowing your student to use his notes as he works. Go over the test together.

Lesson 86

Materials Needed
- Math course of choice

- (optional) *Analytical Grammar,* Student Book and Teacher Book (Schedules A and B)
- *Journaling a Year in Nature* notebooks (optional)

Math: Work on your selected math curriculum for about 30 minutes.

(optional) Analytical Grammar, Schedule A: Go over Unit 6, "Patterns 1 & 2," notes with your student (or use the DVD companion). Do the first two sentences of Unit 6, Exercise 1, together, then assign the remainder to be done independently.

(optional) Analytical Grammar, Schedule B: Go over Unit 4, "Subject & Verb," notes with your student (or use the DVD companion). Do the first two sentences of Unit 4, Exercise 1, together, then assign the remainder to be done independently.

Nature Study: Take the whole family outside for nature study.

Lesson 87

Materials Needed
- *Spelling Wisdom, Book 2*
- *Using Language Well, Book 2, Student Book*
- *Using Language Well, Book 2, Teacher Guide and Answer Key*
- Math course of choice
- (optional) *Analytical Grammar,* Student Book and Teacher Book (Schedule A)

Spelling and Grammar: Complete *Using Language Well, Book 2,* lesson 105.

Math: Work on your selected math curriculum for about 30 minutes.

(optional) Analytical Grammar, Schedule A: Go over the completed Unit 6, Exercise 1, together, then assign Exercise 2 to be done independently.

Reminder: Assign your student to write one narration from his history, geography, Bible, or science readings this week. Use Rubric 2.5 from Using Language Well, Book 2, Teacher Guide and Answer Key *to help you evaluate his writing. Continue oral narrations daily.*

Lesson 88

Materials Needed
- (optional) *Analytical Grammar,* Student Book and Teacher Book (Schedules A and B)
- SCM science course of choice
- Math course of choice

(optional) Analytical Grammar, Schedule A: Go over the completed Unit 6, Exercise 2, together, then assign Exercise 3 to be done independently.

(optional) Analytical Grammar, Schedule B: Go over the completed Unit 4, Exercise 1, together, then assign Exercise 2 to be done independently.

Science: In your SCM science course, complete the first assignment for Week 18.

Math: Work on your selected math curriculum for about 30 minutes.

Lesson 89

Materials Needed
- Typing course of choice
- Math course of choice
- (optional) *Analytical Grammar,* Student Book and Teacher Book (Schedules A and B)

Typing: Work on your selected typing course for about 20 minutes.

Math: Work on your selected math curriculum for about 30 minutes.

(optional) Analytical Grammar, Schedule A: Go over the completed Unit 6, Exercise 3, together. Assign and go over the Skills Support exercise if desired.

(optional) Analytical Grammar, Schedule B: Go over the completed Unit 4, Exercise 2, together, then assign Exercise 3 to be done independently.

Lesson 90

Materials Needed
- SCM science course of choice
- *Spelling Wisdom, Book 2*
- *Using Language Well, Book 2, Student Book*
- *Using Language Well, Book 2, Teacher Guide and Answer Key*
- Math course of choice
- (optional) *Analytical Grammar,* Student Book and Teacher Book (Schedule A)

Science: In your SCM science course, complete the second assignment for Week 18.

Spelling and Grammar: Complete *Using Language Well, Book 2,* lesson 106.

Math: Work on your selected math curriculum for about 30 minutes.

(optional) Analytical Grammar, Schedule A: Assign the Unit 6 test, allowing your student to use his notes as he works. Go over the test together.

Tip: Remind your student to record in his Book of Mottoes any meaningful quotations, poetry, excerpts, or Scripture passages from recent readings (if he is interested in that ongoing project).

Lesson 91

Materials Needed
- Math course of choice
- (optional) *Analytical Grammar,* Student Book and Teacher Book (Schedules A and B)
- *Journaling a Year in Nature* notebooks (optional)

Math: Work on your selected math curriculum for about 30 minutes.

(optional) Analytical Grammar, Schedule A: Go over Unit 7, "Pattern 3," notes with your student (or use the DVD companion). Do the first two sentences of Unit 7, Exercise 1, together, then assign the remainder to be done independently.

(optional) Analytical Grammar, Schedule B: Go over the completed Unit 4, Exercise 3, together. Assign and go over the Skills Support exercise if desired.

Nature Study: Take the whole family outside for nature study.

Reminder: Assign your student to write one narration from his history, geography, Bible, or science readings this week. Use Rubric 2.5 from Using Language Well, Book 2, Teacher Guide and Answer Key *to help you evaluate his writing. Continue oral narrations daily.*

Lesson 92

Materials Needed
- *Spelling Wisdom, Book 2*
- *Using Language Well, Book 2, Student Book*
- *Using Language Well, Book 2, Teacher Guide and Answer Key*
- Math course of choice
- (optional) *Analytical Grammar,* Student Book and Teacher Book (Schedule A)

Spelling and Grammar: Complete *Using Language Well, Book 2,* lesson 107.

Math: Work on your selected math curriculum for about 30 minutes.

(optional) Analytical Grammar, Schedule A: Go over the completed Unit 7, Exercise 1, together, then assign Exercise 2 to be done independently.

Lesson 93

Materials Needed
- (optional) *Analytical Grammar,* Student Book and Teacher Book (Schedules A and B)
- SCM science course of choice
- Math course of choice

(optional) Analytical Grammar, Schedule A: Go over the completed Unit 7, Exercise 2, together, then assign Exercise 3 to be done independently.

(optional) Analytical Grammar, Schedule B: Assign the Unit 4 test, allowing your student to use his notes as he works. Go over the test together.

Science: In your SCM science course, complete the first assignment for Week 19.

Math: Work on your selected math curriculum for about 30 minutes.

Lesson 94

Materials Needed
- Typing course of choice
- Math course of choice
- (optional) *Analytical Grammar,* Student Book and Teacher Book (Schedules A and B)

Typing: Work on your selected typing course for about 20 minutes.

Math: Work on your selected math curriculum for about 30 minutes.

(optional) Analytical Grammar, Schedule A: Go over the completed Unit 7, Exercise 3, together. Assign and go over the Skills Support exercise if desired.

(optional) Analytical Grammar, Schedule B: Go over Unit 5, "Adverbs," notes with your student (or use the DVD companion). Do the first two sentences of Unit 5, Exercise 1, together, then assign the remainder to be done independently.

Lesson 95

Materials Needed
- SCM science course of choice
- *Spelling Wisdom, Book 2*
- *Using Language Well, Book 2, Student Book*
- *Using Language Well, Book 2, Teacher Guide and Answer Key*
- Math course of choice
- (optional) *Analytical Grammar,* Student Book and Teacher Book (Schedule A)

Science: In your SCM science course, complete the second assignment for Week 19.

Spelling and Grammar: Complete *Using Language Well, Book 2,* lesson 108.

Math: Work on your selected math curriculum for about 30 minutes.

(optional) Analytical Grammar, Schedule A: Assign the Unit 7 test, allowing your student to use his notes as he works. Go over the test together.

Lesson 96

Materials Needed
- Math course of choice
- (optional) *Analytical Grammar,* Student Book and Teacher Book (Schedules A and B)
- *Journaling a Year in Nature* notebooks (optional)

Math: Work on your selected math curriculum for about 30 minutes.

(optional) Analytical Grammar, Schedule A: Go over Unit 8, "Linking Verbs and Patterns 4 & 5," notes with your student (or use the DVD companion). Do the first two sentences of Unit 8, Exercise 1, together, then assign the remainder to be done independently.

(optional) Analytical Grammar, Schedule B: Go over the completed Unit 5, Exercise 1, together, then assign Exercise 2 to be done independently.

Nature Study: Take the whole family outside for nature study.

Reminder: Assign your student to write one narration from his history, geography, Bible, or science readings this week. Use Rubric 2.5 from Using Language Well, Book 2, Teacher Guide and Answer Key *to help you evaluate his writing. Continue oral narrations daily.*

Lesson 97

Materials Needed
- *Spelling Wisdom, Book 2*
- *Using Language Well, Book 2, Student Book*
- *Using Language Well, Book 2, Teacher Guide and Answer Key*
- Math course of choice
- (optional) *Analytical Grammar,* Student Book and Teacher Book (Schedule A)

Spelling and Grammar: Complete *Using Language Well, Book 2,* lesson 109.

Math: Work on your selected math curriculum for about 30 minutes.

(optional) Analytical Grammar, Schedule A: Go over the completed Unit 8, Exercise 1, together, then assign Exercise 2 to be done independently.

Lesson 98

Materials Needed
- (optional) *Analytical Grammar,* Student Book and Teacher Book (Schedules A and B)
- SCM science course of choice
- Math course of choice

(optional) Analytical Grammar, Schedule A: Go over the completed Unit 8, Exercise 2, together, then assign Exercise 3 to be done independently.

(optional) Analytical Grammar, Schedule B: Go over the completed Unit 5, Exercise 2, together, then assign Exercise 3 to be done independently.

Science: In your SCM science course, complete the first assignment for Week 20.

Math: Work on your selected math curriculum for about 30 minutes.

Lesson 99

Materials Needed
- Typing course of choice
- Math course of choice
- (optional) *Analytical Grammar,* Student Book and Teacher Book (Schedules A and B)

Typing: Work on your selected typing course for about 20 minutes.

Math: Work on your selected math curriculum for about 30 minutes.

(optional) Analytical Grammar, Schedule A: Go over the completed Unit 8, Exercise 3, together. Assign and go over the Skills Support exercise if desired.

(optional) Analytical Grammar, Schedule B: Go over the completed Unit 5, Exercise 3, together. Assign and go over the Skills Support exercise if desired.

Lesson 100

Materials Needed
- SCM science course of choice
- *Spelling Wisdom, Book 2*
- *Using Language Well, Book 2, Student Book*

- *Using Language Well, Book 2, Teacher Guide and Answer Key*
- Math course of choice
- (optional) *Analytical Grammar,* Student Book and Teacher Book (Schedule A)

Science: In your SCM science course, complete the second assignment for Week 20.

Spelling and Grammar: Complete *Using Language Well, Book 2,* lesson 110.

Math: Work on your selected math curriculum for about 30 minutes.

(optional) Analytical Grammar, Schedule A: Assign the Unit 8 test, allowing your student to use his notes as he works. Go over the test together.

Lesson 101

Materials Needed
- Math course of choice
- (optional) *Analytical Grammar,* Student Book and Teacher Book (Schedules A and B)
- *Journaling a Year in Nature* notebooks (optional)

Math: Work on your selected math curriculum for about 30 minutes.

(optional) Analytical Grammar, Schedule A: Go over Unit 9, "Helping Verbs," notes with your student (or use the DVD companion). Do the first two sentences of Unit 9, Exercise 1, together, then assign the remainder to be done independently.

(optional) Analytical Grammar, Schedule B: Assign the Unit 5 test, allowing your student to use his notes as he works. Go over the test together.

Nature Study: Take the whole family outside for nature study.

Reminder: Assign your student to write one narration from his history, geography, Bible, or science readings this week. Use Rubric 2.5 from Using Language Well, Book 2, Teacher Guide and Answer Key *to help you evaluate his writing. Continue oral narrations daily.*

Lesson 102

Materials Needed
- *Spelling Wisdom, Book 2*
- *Using Language Well, Book 2, Student Book*
- *Using Language Well, Book 2, Teacher Guide and Answer Key*
- Math course of choice

- (optional) *Analytical Grammar,* Student Book and Teacher Book (Schedule A)

Spelling and Grammar: Complete *Using Language Well, Book 2,* lesson 111.

Math: Work on your selected math curriculum for about 30 minutes.

(optional) Analytical Grammar, Schedule A: Go over the completed Unit 9, Exercise 1, together, then assign Exercise 2 to be done independently.

Lesson 103

Materials Needed
- (optional) *Analytical Grammar,* Student Book and Teacher Book (Schedules A and B)
- SCM science course of choice
- Math course of choice

(optional) Analytical Grammar, Schedule A: Go over the completed Unit 9, Exercise 2, together, then assign Exercise 3 to be done independently.

(optional) Analytical Grammar, Schedule B: Go over Unit 6, "Patterns 1 & 2," notes with your student (or use the DVD companion). Do the first two sentences of Unit 6, Exercise 1, together, then assign the remainder to be done independently.

Science: In your SCM science course, complete the first assignment for Week 21.

Math: Work on your selected math curriculum for about 30 minutes.

Lesson 104

Materials Needed
- Typing course of choice
- Math course of choice
- (optional) *Analytical Grammar,* Student Book and Teacher Book (Schedules A and B)

Typing: Work on your selected typing course for about 20 minutes.

Math: Work on your selected math curriculum for about 30 minutes.

(optional) Analytical Grammar, Schedule A: Go over the completed Unit 9, Exercise 3, together. Assign and go over the Skills Support exercise if desired.

(optional) Analytical Grammar, Schedule B: Go over the completed Unit 6, Exercise 1, together, then assign Exercise 2 to be done independently.

Notes

Lesson 105

Materials Needed
- SCM science course of choice
- *Spelling Wisdom, Book 2*
- *Using Language Well, Book 2, Student Book*
- *Using Language Well, Book 2, Teacher Guide and Answer Key*
- Math course of choice
- (optional) *Analytical Grammar,* Student Book and Teacher Book (Schedule A)

Science: In your SCM science course, complete the second assignment for Week 21.

Spelling and Grammar: Complete *Using Language Well, Book 2,* lesson 112.

Math: Work on your selected math curriculum for about 30 minutes.

(optional) Analytical Grammar, Schedule A: Assign the Unit 9 test, allowing your student to use his notes as he works. Go over the test together.

Lesson 106

Materials Needed
- Math course of choice
- (optional) *Analytical Grammar,* Student Book and Teacher Book (Schedules A and B)
- *Journaling a Year in Nature* notebooks (optional)

Math: Work on your selected math curriculum for about 30 minutes.

(optional) Analytical Grammar, Schedule A: Go over Unit 10, "Conjunctions & Compound Situations," notes with your student (or use the DVD companion). Do the first two sentences of Unit 10, Exercise 1, together, then assign the remainder to be done independently.

(optional) Analytical Grammar, Schedule B: Go over the completed Unit 6, Exercise 2, together, then assign Exercise 3 to be done independently.

Nature Study: Take the whole family outside for nature study.

Reminder: Assign your student to write one narration from his history, geography, Bible, or science readings this week. Use Rubric 2.5 from Using Language Well, Book 2, Teacher Guide and Answer Key *to help you evaluate his writing. Continue oral narrations daily.*

Lesson 107

Materials Needed
- *Spelling Wisdom, Book 2*
- *Using Language Well, Book 2, Student Book*
- *Using Language Well, Book 2, Teacher Guide and Answer Key*
- Math course of choice
- (optional) *Analytical Grammar,* Student Book and Teacher Book (Schedule A)

Spelling and Grammar: Complete *Using Language Well, Book 2,* lesson 113.

Math: Work on your selected math curriculum for about 30 minutes.

(optional) Analytical Grammar, Schedule A: Go over the completed Unit 10, Exercise 1, together, then assign Exercise 2 to be done independently.

Lesson 108

Materials Needed
- (optional) *Analytical Grammar,* Student Book and Teacher Book (Schedules A and B)
- SCM science course of choice
- Math course of choice

(optional) Analytical Grammar, Schedule A: Go over the completed Unit 10, Exercise 2, together, then assign Exercise 3 to be done independently.

(optional) Analytical Grammar, Schedule B: Go over the completed Unit 6, Exercise 3, together. Assign and go over the Skills Support exercise if desired.

Science: In your SCM science course, complete the first assignment for Week 22.

Math: Work on your selected math curriculum for about 30 minutes.

Lesson 109

Materials Needed
- Typing course of choice
- Math course of choice
- (optional) *Analytical Grammar,* Student Book and Teacher Book (Schedules A and B)

Typing: Work on your selected typing course for about 20 minutes.

Math: Work on your selected math curriculum for about 30 minutes.

(optional) Analytical Grammar, Schedule A: Go over the completed Unit 10,

Exercise 3, together. Assign and go over the Skills Support exercise if desired.

(optional) Analytical Grammar, Schedule B: Assign the Unit 6 test, allowing your student to use his notes as he works. Go over the test together.

Lesson 110

Materials Needed
- SCM science course of choice
- *Spelling Wisdom, Book 2*
- *Using Language Well, Book 2, Student Book*
- *Using Language Well, Book 2, Teacher Guide and Answer Key*
- Math course of choice
- (optional) *Analytical Grammar,* Student Book and Teacher Book (Schedule A)

Science: In your SCM science course, complete the second assignment for Week 22.

Spelling and Grammar: Complete *Using Language Well, Book 2,* lesson 114.

Math: Work on your selected math curriculum for about 30 minutes.

(optional) Analytical Grammar, Schedule A: Assign the Unit 10 test, allowing your student to use his notes as he works. Go over the test together.

Lesson 111

Materials Needed
- Math course of choice
- (optional) *Analytical Grammar,* Student Book and Teacher Book (Schedule B)
- *Journaling a Year in Nature* notebooks (optional)

Math: Work on your selected math curriculum for about 30 minutes.

(optional) Analytical Grammar, Schedule B: Go over Unit 7, "Pattern 3," notes with your student (or use the DVD companion). Do the first two sentences of Unit 7, Exercise 1, together, then assign the remainder to be done independently.

Nature Study: Take the whole family outside for nature study.

Reminder: Assign your student to write one narration from his history, geography, Bible, or science readings this week. Use Rubric 2.5 from Using Language Well, Book 2, Teacher Guide and Answer Key *to help you evaluate his writing. Continue oral narrations daily.*

Lesson 112

Materials Needed
- *Spelling Wisdom, Book 2*
- *Using Language Well, Book 2, Student Book*
- *Using Language Well, Book 2, Teacher Guide and Answer Key*
- Math course of choice

Spelling and Grammar: Complete *Using Language Well, Book 2,* lesson 115.

Math: Work on your selected math curriculum for about 30 minutes.

Lesson 113

Materials Needed
- (optional) *Analytical Grammar,* Student Book and Teacher Book (Schedule B)
- SCM science course of choice
- Math course of choice

(optional) Analytical Grammar, Schedule B: Go over the completed Unit 7, Exercise 1, together, then assign Exercise 2 to be done independently.

Science: In your SCM science course, complete the first assignment for Week 23.

Math: Work on your selected math curriculum for about 30 minutes.

Lesson 114

Materials Needed
- Typing course of choice
- Math course of choice
- (optional) *Analytical Grammar,* Student Book and Teacher Book (Schedule B)

Typing: Work on your selected typing course for about 20 minutes.

Math: Work on your selected math curriculum for about 30 minutes.

(optional) Analytical Grammar, Schedule B: Go over the completed Unit 7, Exercise 2, together, then assign Exercise 3 to be done independently.

Lesson 115

Materials Needed
- SCM science course of choice
- *Spelling Wisdom, Book 2*

- *Using Language Well, Book 2, Student Book*
- *Using Language Well, Book 2, Teacher Guide and Answer Key*
- Math course of choice

Science: In your SCM science course, complete the second assignment for Week 23.

Spelling and Grammar: Complete *Using Language Well, Book 2,* lesson 116.

Math: Work on your selected math curriculum for about 30 minutes.

Lesson 116

Materials Needed
- Math course of choice
- (optional) *Analytical Grammar,* Student Book and Teacher Book (Schedule B)
- *Journaling a Year in Nature* notebooks (optional)

Math: Work on your selected math curriculum for about 30 minutes.

(optional) Analytical Grammar, Schedule B: Go over the completed Unit 7, Exercise 3, together. Assign and go over the Skills Support exercise if desired.

Nature Study: Take the whole family outside for nature study.

Reminder: Assign your student to write one narration from his history, geography, Bible, or science readings this week. Use Rubric 2.5 from Using Language Well, Book 2, Teacher Guide and Answer Key *to help you evaluate his writing. Continue oral narrations daily.*

Lesson 117

Materials Needed
- *Spelling Wisdom, Book 2*
- *Using Language Well, Book 2, Student Book*
- *Using Language Well, Book 2, Teacher Guide and Answer Key*
- Math course of choice

Spelling and Grammar: Complete *Using Language Well, Book 2,* lesson 117.

Math: Work on your selected math curriculum for about 30 minutes.

Lesson 118

Materials Needed
- (optional) *Analytical Grammar,* Student Book and Teacher Book (Schedule B)

- SCM science course of choice
- Math course of choice

(optional) Analytical Grammar, Schedule B: Assign the Unit 7 test, allowing your student to use his notes as he works. Go over the test together.

Science: In your SCM science course, complete the first assignment for Week 24.

Math: Work on your selected math curriculum for about 30 minutes.

Lesson 119

Materials Needed
- Typing course of choice
- Math course of choice
- (optional) *Analytical Grammar,* Student Book and Teacher Book (Schedule B)

Typing: Work on your selected typing course for about 20 minutes.

Math: Work on your selected math curriculum for about 30 minutes.

(optional) Analytical Grammar, Schedule B: Use today to catch up on any assignments in *Analytical Grammar* so far.

Lesson 120

Materials Needed
- SCM science course of choice
- *Spelling Wisdom,* Book 2
- *Using Language Well,* Book 2, Student Book
- *Using Language Well,* Book 2, Teacher Guide and Answer Key
- Math course of choice

Science: In your SCM science course, complete the second assignment for Week 24.

Spelling and Grammar: Complete *Using Language Well, Book 2,* lesson 118.

Math: Work on your selected math curriculum for about 30 minutes.

Tip: Remind your student to record in his Book of Mottoes any meaningful quotations, poetry, excerpts, or Scripture passages from recent readings (if he is interested in that ongoing project).

Term 3

(12 weeks; 5 lessons/week)

Term 3 Resources List

- *Spelling Wisdom, Book 2*
- *Using Language Well, Book 2, Student Book*
- *Using Language Well, Book 2, Teacher Guide and Answer Key*
- (optional) *Analytical Grammar,* Student Book and Teacher Book (Schedule B only)
- Simply Charlotte Mason (SCM) science course of choice
- *Journaling a Year in Nature* notebooks (optional)
- Typing course of choice
- Math course of choice

Weekly Schedule *(most weeks)*

	Day One	Day Two	Day Three	Day Four	Day Five
	Math (20–30 min.)	Math (20–30 min.)	Math (20–30 min.)	Math (20–30 min.)	Math (20–30 min.)
		Science (20–30 min.)		(Nature Study)	Science (20–30 min.)
	Typing (15–20 min.)	Spelling Wisdom & Using Language Well (20–30 min.)		Spelling Wisdom & Using Language Well (20–30 min.)	
Schedule B	(opt.) Analytical Grammar		(opt.) Analytical Grammar		(opt.) Analytical Grammar

Lesson 121

Materials Needed
- Math course of choice
- (optional) *Analytical Grammar,* Student Book and Teacher Book (Schedule B)
- Typing course of choice

Math: Work on your selected math curriculum for about 30 minutes.

(optional) Analytical Grammar, Schedule B: Go over Unit 8, "Linking Verbs and Patterns 4 & 5," notes with your student (or use the DVD companion). Do the first two sentences of Unit 8, Exercise 1, together, then assign the remainder to be done independently.

Typing: Work on your selected typing course for about 20 minutes.

Reminder: Assign your student to write one narration from his history, geography, Bible, or science readings this week. Use Rubric 2.5 from Using Language Well, Book 2, Teacher Guide and Answer Key *to help you evaluate his writing. Continue oral narrations daily.*

Lesson 122

Materials Needed
- SCM science course of choice
- Math course of choice
- *Spelling Wisdom, Book 2*
- *Using Language Well, Book 2, Student Book*
- *Using Language Well, Book 2, Teacher Guide and Answer Key*

Science: In your SCM science course, complete the first assignment for Week 25.

Math: Work on your selected math curriculum for about 30 minutes.

Spelling and Grammar: Complete *Using Language Well, Book 2,* lesson 119.

Lesson 123

Materials Needed
- (optional) *Analytical Grammar,* Student Book and Teacher Book (Schedule B)
- Math course of choice

(optional) Analytical Grammar, Schedule B: Go over the completed Unit 8, Exercise 1, together, then assign Exercise 2 to be done independently.

Math: Work on your selected math curriculum for about 30 minutes.

Lesson 124

Materials Needed
- *Spelling Wisdom, Book 2*
- *Using Language Well, Book 2, Student Book*
- *Using Language Well, Book 2, Teacher Guide and Answer Key*
- Math course of choice
- *Journaling a Year in Nature* notebooks (optional)

Spelling and Grammar: Complete *Using Language Well, Book 2,* lesson 120.

Math: Work on your selected math curriculum for about 30 minutes.

Nature Study: Take the whole family outside for nature study.

Lesson 125

Materials Needed
- SCM science course of choice
- (optional) *Analytical Grammar,* Student Book and Teacher Book (Schedule B)
- Math course of choice

Science: In your SCM science course, complete the second assignment for Week 25.

(optional) Analytical Grammar, Schedule B: Go over the completed Unit 8, Exercise 2, together, then assign Exercise 3 to be done independently.

Math: Work on your selected math curriculum for about 30 minutes.

Lesson 126

Materials Needed
- Math course of choice
- (optional) *Analytical Grammar,* Student Book and Teacher Book (Schedule B)
- Typing course of choice

Math: Work on your selected math curriculum for about 30 minutes.

(optional) Analytical Grammar, Schedule B: Go over the completed Unit 8, Exercise 3, together. Assign and go over the Skills Support exercise if desired.

Typing: Work on your selected typing course for about 20 minutes.

Reminder: Assign your student to write one narration from his history, geography, Bible, or science readings this week. Use Rubric 2.5 from Using Language Well, Book 2, Teacher Guide and Answer Key to help you evaluate his writing. Continue oral narrations daily.

Lesson 127

Materials Needed
- SCM science course of choice
- Math course of choice
- *Spelling Wisdom, Book 2*
- *Using Language Well, Book 2, Student Book*
- *Using Language Well, Book 2, Teacher Guide and Answer Key*

Science: In your SCM science course, complete the first assignment for Week 26.

Math: Work on your selected math curriculum for about 30 minutes.

Spelling and Grammar: Complete *Using Language Well, Book 2,* lesson 121.

Lesson 128

Materials Needed
- (optional) *Analytical Grammar,* Student Book and Teacher Book (Schedule B)
- Math course of choice

(optional) Analytical Grammar, Schedule B: Assign the Unit 8 test, allowing your student to use his notes as he works. Go over the test together.

Math: Work on your selected math curriculum for about 30 minutes.

Lesson 129

Materials Needed
- *Spelling Wisdom, Book 2*
- *Using Language Well, Book 2, Student Book*
- *Using Language Well, Book 2, Teacher Guide and Answer Key*
- Math course of choice
- *Journaling a Year in Nature* notebooks (optional)

Spelling and Grammar: Complete *Using Language Well, Book 2,* lesson 122.

Math: Work on your selected math curriculum for about 30 minutes.

Nature Study: Take the whole family outside for nature study.

Lesson 130

Materials Needed
- SCM science course of choice
- (optional) *Analytical Grammar,* Student Book and Teacher Book (Schedule B)
- Math course of choice

Science: In your SCM science course, complete the second assignment for Week 26.

(optional) Analytical Grammar, Schedule B: Go over Unit 9, "Helping Verbs," notes with your student (or use the DVD companion). Do the first two sentences of Unit 9, Exercise 1, together, then assign the remainder to be done independently.

Math: Work on your selected math curriculum for about 30 minutes.

Lesson 131

Materials Needed
- Math course of choice
- (optional) *Analytical Grammar,* Student Book and Teacher Book (Schedule B)
- Typing course of choice

Math: Work on your selected math curriculum for about 30 minutes.

(optional) Analytical Grammar, Schedule B: Go over the completed Unit 9, Exercise 1, together, then assign Exercise 2 to be done independently.

Typing: Work on your selected typing course for about 20 minutes.

Reminder: Assign your student to write one narration from his history, geography, Bible, or science readings this week. Use Rubric 2.5 from Using Language Well, Book 2, Teacher Guide and Answer Key *to help you evaluate his writing. Continue oral narrations daily.*

Lesson 132

Materials Needed
- SCM science course of choice
- Math course of choice
- *Spelling Wisdom, Book 2*
- *Using Language Well, Book 2, Student Book*
- *Using Language Well, Book 2, Teacher Guide and Answer Key*

Science: In your SCM science course, complete the first assignment for Week 27.

Math: Work on your selected math curriculum for about 30 minutes.

Spelling and Grammar: Complete *Using Language Well, Book 2,* lesson 123.

Tip: Remind your student to record in his Book of Mottoes any meaningful quotations, poetry, excerpts, or Scripture passages from recent readings (if he is interested in that ongoing project).

Lesson 133

Materials Needed
- (optional) *Analytical Grammar,* Student Book and Teacher Book (Schedule B)
- Math course of choice

(optional) Analytical Grammar, Schedule B: Go over the completed Unit 9, Exercise 2, together, then assign Exercise 3 to be done independently.

Math: Work on your selected math curriculum for about 30 minutes.

Lesson 134

Materials Needed
- *Spelling Wisdom, Book 2*
- *Using Language Well, Book 2, Student Book*
- *Using Language Well, Book 2, Teacher Guide and Answer Key*
- Math course of choice
- *Journaling a Year in Nature* notebooks (optional)

Spelling and Grammar: Complete *Using Language Well, Book 2,* lesson 124.

Math: Work on your selected math curriculum for about 30 minutes.

Nature Study: Take the whole family outside for nature study.

Lesson 135

Materials Needed
- SCM science course of choice
- (optional) *Analytical Grammar,* Student Book and Teacher Book (Schedule B)
- Math course of choice

Science: In your SCM science course, complete the second assignment for Week 27.

(optional) Analytical Grammar, Schedule B: Go over the completed Unit 9, Exercise 3, together. Assign and go over the Skills Support exercise if desired.

Math: Work on your selected math curriculum for about 30 minutes.

Lesson 136

Materials Needed
- Math course of choice
- (optional) *Analytical Grammar,* Student Book and Teacher Book (Schedule B)
- Typing course of choice

Math: Work on your selected math curriculum for about 30 minutes.

(optional) Analytical Grammar, Schedule B: Assign the Unit 9 test, allowing your student to use his notes as he works. Go over the test together.

Typing: Work on your selected typing course for about 20 minutes.

Reminder: Assign your student to write one narration from his history, geography, Bible, or science readings this week. Use Rubric 2.5 from Using Language Well, Book 2, Teacher Guide and Answer Key *to help you evaluate his writing. Continue oral narrations daily.*

Lesson 137

Materials Needed
- SCM science course of choice
- Math course of choice
- *Spelling Wisdom, Book 2*
- *Using Language Well, Book 2, Student Book*
- *Using Language Well, Book 2, Teacher Guide and Answer Key*

Science: In your SCM science course, complete the first assignment for Week 28.

Math: Work on your selected math curriculum for about 30 minutes.

Spelling and Grammar: Complete *Using Language Well, Book 2,* lesson 125.

Lesson 138

Materials Needed
- (optional) *Analytical Grammar,* Student Book and Teacher Book (Schedule B)
- Math course of choice

(optional) Analytical Grammar, Schedule B: Go over Unit 10, "Conjunctions & Compound Situations," notes with your student (or use the DVD companion). Do the first two sentences of Unit 10, Exercise 1, together, then assign the remainder to be done independently.

Math: Work on your selected math curriculum for about 30 minutes.

Lesson 139

Materials Needed
- *Spelling Wisdom, Book 2*
- *Using Language Well, Book 2, Student Book*
- *Using Language Well, Book 2, Teacher Guide and Answer Key*
- Math course of choice
- *Journaling a Year in Nature* notebooks (optional)

Spelling and Grammar: Complete *Using Language Well, Book 2,* lesson 126.

Math: Work on your selected math curriculum for about 30 minutes.

Nature Study: Take the whole family outside for nature study.

Lesson 140

Materials Needed
- SCM science course of choice
- (optional) *Analytical Grammar,* Student Book and Teacher Book (Schedule B)
- Math course of choice

Science: In your SCM science course, complete the second assignment for Week 28.

(optional) Analytical Grammar, Schedule B: Go over the completed Unit 10, Exercise 1, together, then assign Exercise 2 to be done independently.

Math: Work on your selected math curriculum for about 30 minutes.

Lesson 141

Materials Needed
- Math course of choice
- (optional) *Analytical Grammar,* Student Book and Teacher Book (Schedule B)
- Typing course of choice

Math: Work on your selected math curriculum for about 30 minutes.

(optional) Analytical Grammar, Schedule B: Go over the completed Unit 10, Exercise 2, together, then assign Exercise 3 to be done independently.

Typing: Work on your selected typing course for about 20 minutes.

Reminder: Assign your student to write one narration from his history, geography, Bible, or science readings this week. Use Rubric 2.5 from Using Language Well, Book 2, Teacher Guide and Answer Key *to help you evaluate his writing. Continue oral narrations daily.*

Lesson 142

Materials Needed
- SCM science course of choice
- Math course of choice
- *Spelling Wisdom, Book 2*
- *Using Language Well, Book 2, Student Book*
- *Using Language Well, Book 2, Teacher Guide and Answer Key*

Science: In your SCM science course, complete the first assignment for Week 29.

Math: Work on your selected math curriculum for about 30 minutes.

Spelling and Grammar: Complete *Using Language Well, Book 2,* lesson 127.

Lesson 143

Materials Needed
- (optional) *Analytical Grammar,* Student Book and Teacher Book (Schedule B)
- Math course of choice

(optional) Analytical Grammar, Schedule B: Go over the completed Unit 10, Exercise 3, together. Assign and go over the Skills Support exercise if desired.

Math: Work on your selected math curriculum for about 30 minutes.

Lesson 144

Materials Needed
- *Spelling Wisdom, Book 2*
- *Using Language Well, Book 2, Student Book*
- *Using Language Well, Book 2, Teacher Guide and Answer Key*
- Math course of choice
- *Journaling a Year in Nature* notebooks (optional)

Spelling and Grammar: Complete *Using Language Well, Book 2,* lesson 128.

Math: Work on your selected math curriculum for about 30 minutes.

Nature Study: Take the whole family outside for nature study.

Lesson 145

Materials Needed
- SCM science course of choice
- (optional) *Analytical Grammar,* Student Book and Teacher Book (Schedule B)
- Math course of choice

Science: In your SCM science course, complete the second assignment for Week 29.

(optional) Analytical Grammar, Schedule B: Assign the Unit 10 test, allowing your student to use his notes as he works. Go over the test together.

Math: Work on your selected math curriculum for about 30 minutes.

Lesson 146

Materials Needed
- Math course of choice
- Typing course of choice

Math: Work on your selected math curriculum for about 30 minutes.

Typing: Work on your selected typing course for about 20 minutes.

Reminder: Assign your student to write one narration from his history, geography, Bible, or science readings this week. Use Rubric 2.5 from Using Language Well, Book 2, Teacher Guide and Answer Key *to help you evaluate his writing. Continue oral narrations daily.*

Lesson 147

Materials Needed
- SCM science course of choice
- Math course of choice
- *Spelling Wisdom, Book 2*
- *Using Language Well, Book 2, Student Book*
- *Using Language Well, Book 2, Teacher Guide and Answer Key*

Science: In your SCM science course, complete the first assignment for Week 30.

Math: Work on your selected math curriculum for about 30 minutes.

Spelling and Grammar: Complete *Using Language Well, Book 2,* lesson 129.

Tip: Remind your student to record in his Book of Mottoes any meaningful quotations, poetry, excerpts, or Scripture passages from recent readings (if he is interested in that ongoing project).

Lesson 148

Materials Needed
- Math course of choice

Math: Work on your selected math curriculum for about 30 minutes.

Lesson 149

Materials Needed
- *Spelling Wisdom, Book 2*
- *Using Language Well, Book 2, Student Book*
- *Using Language Well, Book 2, Teacher Guide and Answer Key*
- Math course of choice
- *Journaling a Year in Nature* notebooks (optional)

Spelling and Grammar: Complete *Using Language Well, Book 2,* lesson 130.

Math: Work on your selected math curriculum for about 30 minutes.

Nature Study: Take the whole family outside for nature study.

Lesson 150

Materials Needed
- SCM science course of choice
- Math course of choice

Science: In your SCM science course, complete the second assignment for Week 30.

Math: Work on your selected math curriculum for about 30 minutes.

Lesson 151

Materials Needed
- Math course of choice
- Typing course of choice

Math: Work on your selected math curriculum for about 30 minutes.

Typing: Work on your selected typing course for about 20 minutes.

Reminder: Assign your student to write one narration from his history, geography, Bible, or science readings this week. Use Rubric 2.5 from Using Language Well, Book 2, Teacher Guide and Answer Key *to help you evaluate his writing. Continue oral narrations daily.*

Lesson 152

Materials Needed
- SCM science course of choice
- Math course of choice
- *Spelling Wisdom, Book 2*
- *Using Language Well, Book 2, Student Book*
- *Using Language Well, Book 2, Teacher Guide and Answer Key*

Science: In your SCM science course, complete the first assignment for Week 31.

Math: Work on your selected math curriculum for about 30 minutes.

Spelling and Grammar: Complete *Using Language Well, Book 2,* lesson 131.

Lesson 153

Materials Needed
- Math course of choice

Math: Work on your selected math curriculum for about 30 minutes.

Lesson 154

Materials Needed
- *Spelling Wisdom, Book 2*
- *Using Language Well, Book 2, Student Book*
- *Using Language Well, Book 2, Teacher Guide and Answer Key*
- Math course of choice
- *Journaling a Year in Nature* notebooks (optional)

Spelling and Grammar: Complete *Using Language Well, Book 2,* lesson 132.

Math: Work on your selected math curriculum for about 30 minutes.

Nature Study: Take the whole family outside for nature study.

Lesson 155

Materials Needed
- SCM science course of choice
- Math course of choice

Science: In your SCM science course, complete the second assignment for Week 31.

Math: Work on your selected math curriculum for about 30 minutes.

Lesson 156

Materials Needed
- Math course of choice
- Typing course of choice

Math: Work on your selected math curriculum for about 30 minutes.

Typing: Work on your selected typing course for about 20 minutes.

Reminder: Assign your student to write one narration from his history, geography, Bible, or science readings this week. Use Rubric 2.5 from Using Language Well, Book 2, Teacher Guide and Answer Key *to help you evaluate his writing. Continue oral narrations daily.*

Lesson 157

Materials Needed
- SCM science course of choice
- Math course of choice
- *Spelling Wisdom, Book 2*
- *Using Language Well, Book 2, Student Book*
- *Using Language Well, Book 2, Teacher Guide and Answer Key*

Science: In your SCM science course, complete the first assignment for Week 32.

Math: Work on your selected math curriculum for about 30 minutes.

Spelling and Grammar: Complete *Using Language Well, Book 2,* lesson 133.

Lesson 158

Materials Needed
- Math course of choice

Math: Work on your selected math curriculum for about 30 minutes.

Lesson 159

Materials Needed
- *Spelling Wisdom, Book 2*
- *Using Language Well, Book 2, Student Book*
- *Using Language Well, Book 2, Teacher Guide and Answer Key*
- Math course of choice
- *Journaling a Year in Nature* notebooks (optional)

Spelling and Grammar: Complete *Using Language Well, Book 2,* lesson 134.

Math: Work on your selected math curriculum for about 30 minutes.

Nature Study: Take the whole family outside for nature study.

Lesson 160

Materials Needed
- SCM science course of choice
- Math course of choice

Science: In your SCM science course, complete the second assignment for Week 32.

Math: Work on your selected math curriculum for about 30 minutes.

Lesson 161

Materials Needed
- Math course of choice
- Typing course of choice

Math: Work on your selected math curriculum for about 30 minutes.

Typing: Work on your selected typing course for about 20 minutes.

Reminder: Assign your student to write one narration from his history, geography, Bible, or science readings this week. Use Rubric 2.5 from Using Language Well, Book 2, Teacher Guide and Answer Key *to help you evaluate his writing. Continue oral narrations daily.*

Lesson 162

Materials Needed
- SCM science course of choice
- Math course of choice

- *Spelling Wisdom, Book 2*
- *Using Language Well, Book 2, Student Book*
- *Using Language Well, Book 2, Teacher Guide and Answer Key*

Science: In your SCM science course, complete the first assignment for Week 33.

Math: Work on your selected math curriculum for about 30 minutes.

Spelling and Grammar: Complete *Using Language Well, Book 2,* lesson 135.

Tip: Remind your student to record in his Book of Mottoes any meaningful quotations, poetry, excerpts, or Scripture passages from recent readings (if he is interested in that ongoing project).

Lesson 163

Materials Needed
- Math course of choice

Math: Work on your selected math curriculum for about 30 minutes.

Lesson 164

Materials Needed
- *Spelling Wisdom, Book 2*
- *Using Language Well, Book 2, Student Book*
- *Using Language Well, Book 2, Teacher Guide and Answer Key*
- Math course of choice
- *Journaling a Year in Nature* notebooks (optional)

Spelling and Grammar: Complete *Using Language Well, Book 2,* lesson 136.

Math: Work on your selected math curriculum for about 30 minutes.

Nature Study: Take the whole family outside for nature study.

Lesson 165

Materials Needed
- SCM science course of choice
- Math course of choice

Science: In your SCM science course, complete the second assignment for Week 33.

Math: Work on your selected math curriculum for about 30 minutes.

Lesson 166

Materials Needed
- Math course of choice
- Typing course of choice

Math: Work on your selected math curriculum for about 30 minutes.

Typing: Work on your selected typing course for about 20 minutes.

Reminder: Assign your student to write one narration from his history, geography, Bible, or science readings this week. Use Rubric 2.5 from Using Language Well, Book 2, Teacher Guide and Answer Key *to help you evaluate his writing. Continue oral narrations daily.*

Lesson 167

Materials Needed
- SCM science course of choice
- Math course of choice
- *Spelling Wisdom, Book 2*
- *Using Language Well, Book 2, Student Book*
- *Using Language Well, Book 2, Teacher Guide and Answer Key*

Science: In your SCM science course, complete the first assignment for Week 34.

Math: Work on your selected math curriculum for about 30 minutes.

Spelling and Grammar: Complete *Using Language Well, Book 2,* lesson 137.

Lesson 168

Materials Needed
- Math course of choice

Math: Work on your selected math curriculum for about 30 minutes.

Lesson 169

Materials Needed
- *Spelling Wisdom, Book 2*
- *Using Language Well, Book 2, Student Book*
- *Using Language Well, Book 2, Teacher Guide and Answer Key*
- Math course of choice
- *Journaling a Year in Nature* notebooks (optional)

Notes

Spelling and Grammar: Complete *Using Language Well, Book 2,* lesson 138.

Math: Work on your selected math curriculum for about 30 minutes.

Nature Study: Take the whole family outside for nature study.

Lesson 170

Materials Needed
- SCM science course of choice
- Math course of choice

Science: In your SCM science course, complete the second assignment for Week 34.

Math: Work on your selected math curriculum for about 30 minutes.

Lesson 171

Materials Needed
- Math course of choice
- Typing course of choice

Math: Work on your selected math curriculum for about 30 minutes.

Typing: Work on your selected typing course for about 20 minutes.

Reminder: Assign your student to write one narration from his history, geography, Bible, or science readings this week. Use Rubric 2.5 from Using Language Well, Book 2, Teacher Guide and Answer Key *to help you evaluate his writing. Continue oral narrations daily.*

Lesson 172

Materials Needed
- SCM science course of choice
- Math course of choice
- *Spelling Wisdom, Book 2*
- *Using Language Well, Book 2, Student Book*
- *Using Language Well, Book 2, Teacher Guide and Answer Key*

Science: In your SCM science course, complete the first assignment for Week 35.

Math: Work on your selected math curriculum for about 30 minutes.

Spelling and Grammar: Complete *Using Language Well, Book 2,* lesson 139.

Lesson 173

Materials Needed
- Math course of choice

Math: Work on your selected math curriculum for about 30 minutes.

Lesson 174

Materials Needed
- *Spelling Wisdom, Book 2*
- *Using Language Well, Book 2, Student Book*
- *Using Language Well, Book 2, Teacher Guide and Answer Key*
- Math course of choice
- *Journaling a Year in Nature* notebooks (optional)

Spelling and Grammar: Complete *Using Language Well, Book 2,* lesson 140.

Math: Work on your selected math curriculum for about 30 minutes.

Nature Study: Take the whole family outside for nature study.

Lesson 175

Materials Needed
- SCM science course of choice
- Math course of choice

Science: In your SCM science course, complete the second assignment for Week 35.

Math: Work on your selected math curriculum for about 30 minutes.

Lesson 176

Materials Needed
- Math course of choice
- Typing course of choice

Math: Work on your selected math curriculum for about 30 minutes.

Typing: Work on your selected typing course for about 20 minutes.

Reminder: Assign your student to write one narration from his history, geography, Bible, or science readings this week. Use Rubric 2.5 from Using Language Well, Book 2, Teacher Guide and Answer Key *to help you evaluate his writing. Continue oral narrations daily.*

Notes

Lesson 177

Materials Needed
- SCM science course of choice
- Math course of choice
- *Spelling Wisdom, Book 2*
- *Using Language Well, Book 2, Student Book*
- *Using Language Well, Book 2, Teacher Guide and Answer Key*

Science: In your SCM science course, complete the first assignment for Week 36.

Math: Work on your selected math curriculum for about 30 minutes.

Spelling and Grammar: Use today and lesson 179 to catch up on any assignments in *Using Language Well, Book 2*, as needed.

Tip: Remind your student to record in his Book of Mottoes any meaningful quotations, poetry, excerpts, or Scripture passages from recent readings (if he is interested in that ongoing project).

Lesson 178

Materials Needed
- Math course of choice

Math: Work on your selected math curriculum for about 30 minutes.

Lesson 179

Materials Needed
- *Spelling Wisdom, Book 2*
- *Using Language Well, Book 2, Student Book*
- *Using Language Well, Book 2, Teacher Guide and Answer Key*
- Math course of choice
- *Journaling a Year in Nature* notebooks (optional)

Spelling and Grammar: Use today to catch up on any assignments in *Using Language Well, Book 2,* as needed.

Math: Work on your selected math curriculum for about 30 minutes.

Nature Study: Take the whole family outside for nature study.

Lesson 180

Materials Needed
- SCM science course of choice
- Math course of choice

Science: In your SCM science course, complete the second assignment for Week 36.

Math: Work on your selected math curriculum for about 30 minutes.